Disney
FOR TEEN SINGERS
YOUNG WOMEN'S EDITION
35 Classic and Contemporary Songs

ISBN 978-1-4950-0997-6

Walt Disney Music Company
Wonderland Music Company, Inc.

DISTRIBUTED BY

HAL•LEONARD®
CORPORATION

7777 W. BLUEMOUND RD. P.O. BOX 13819 MILWAUKEE, WI 53213

The following songs are property of:
Bourne Co.
Music Publishers
5 West 37th Street
New York, NY 10018

WHEN YOU WISH UPON A STAR
WITH A SMILE AND A SONG

Visit Hal Leonard Online at
www.halleonard.com

CONTENTS

ALICE

from Walt Disney Pictures' *Alice in Wonderland - A Film by Tim Burton*

Words and Music by
Avril Lavigne

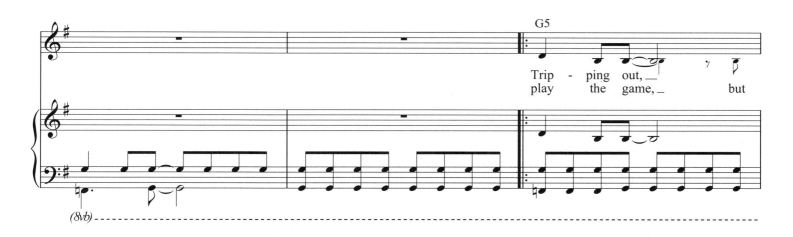

Trip - ping out,_ _____
play the game,_ but

spin-ning a - round._ I'm un - der - ground; I _____ fell down,_____
I can't_ stay._ I've got my head on straight, and I'm_ not gon - na change,

oh.

no.

I,

(8vb)

loco

Am7 G F(add#4)

I'll get by.

C Am7 G

I, I'll sur - vive.

F C Am7

When the world's crash-ing down, when I fall and hit the ground,

I will turn my-self a-round; don't you try to stop me. I,

I won't cry.

I'll

I

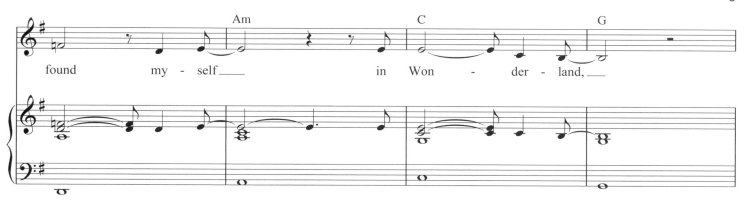

found my - self ___ in Won - der - land, ___

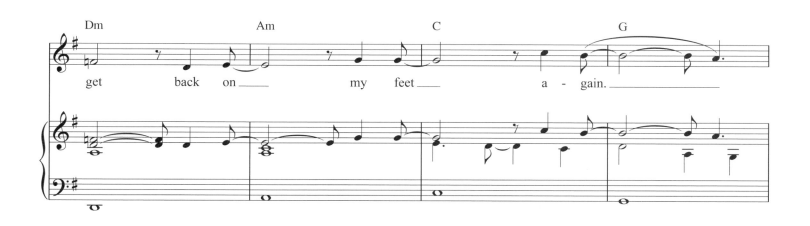

get back on ___ my feet ___ a - gain. ___

Is ___ this real? ___ Is it ___ pre - tend? ___ I'll

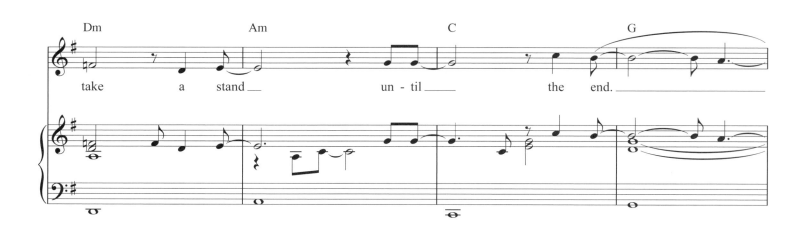

take a stand ___ un - til ___ the end. ___

I, _____ I'll get _

G   F(add#4)   C

by. _____ I, _____

Am7   G   F

I'll sur - vive. _____

C   Am7   G

When the world's crash-ing down, __ when I fall and hit the ground, __ I will turn my-self a-round;

don't you try to stop me. I,_____ I won't_

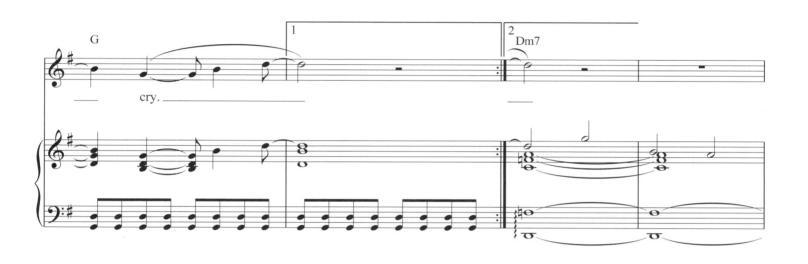

cry._____

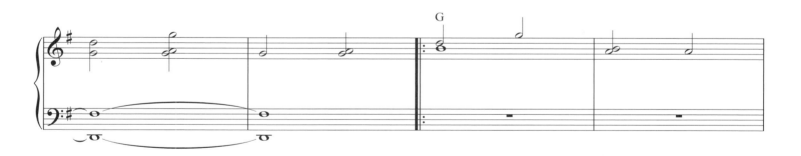

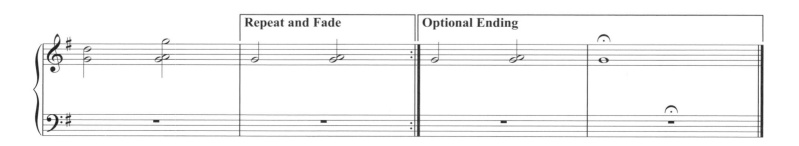

Repeat and Fade   **Optional Ending**

BEAUTY AND THE BEAST
from Walt Disney's *Beauty and the Beast: The Broadway Musical*

Lyrics by Howard Ashman
Music by Alan Menken

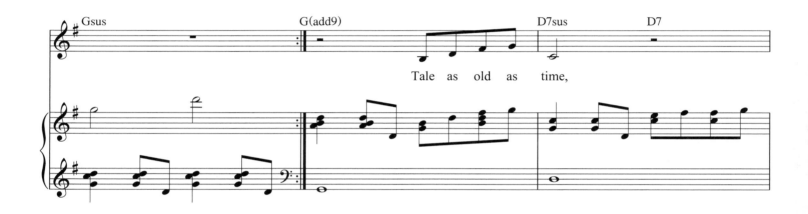

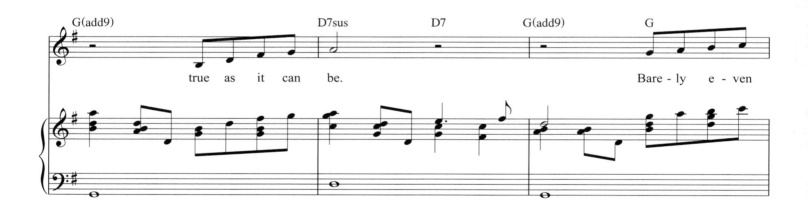

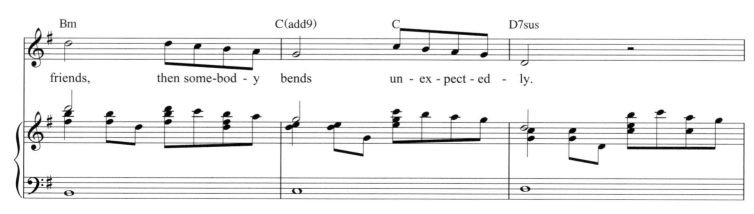

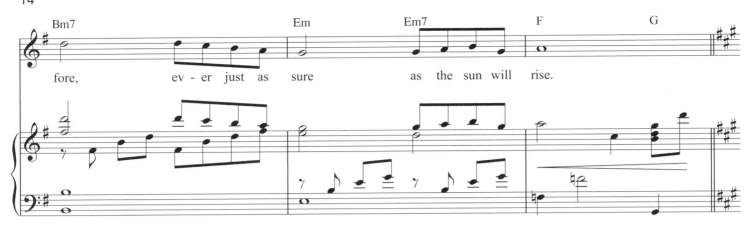

fore, ev - er just as sure as the sun will rise.

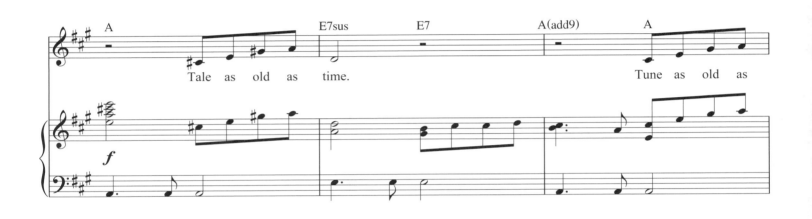

Tale as old as time. Tune as old as

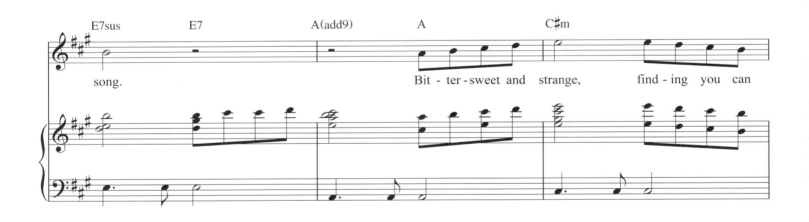

song. Bit - ter - sweet and strange, find - ing you can

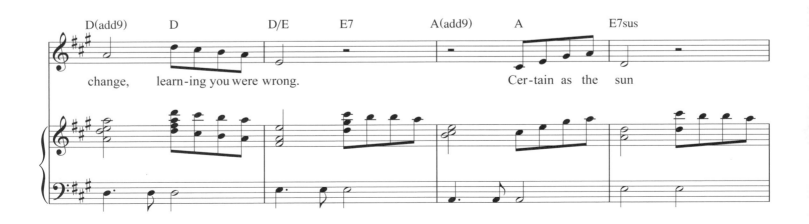

change, learn-ing you were wrong. Cer-tain as the sun

BELLE
(Reprise)
from Walt Disney's *Beauty and the Beast*

Lyrics by Howard Ashman
Music by Alan Menken

Brightly

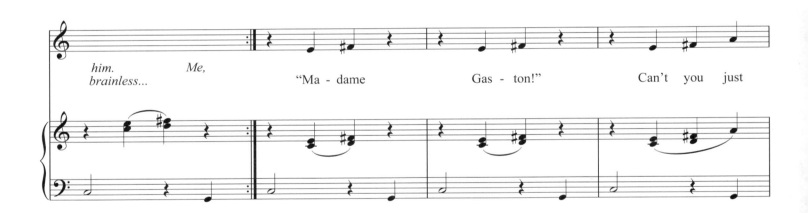

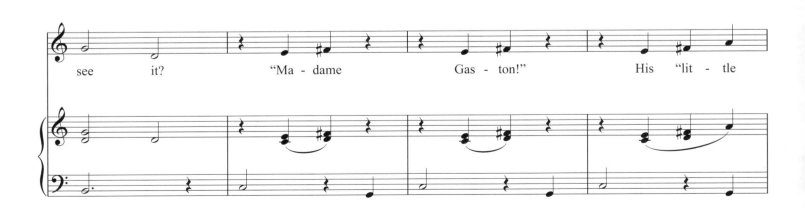

wife." No, sir. Not me! I guar - an -

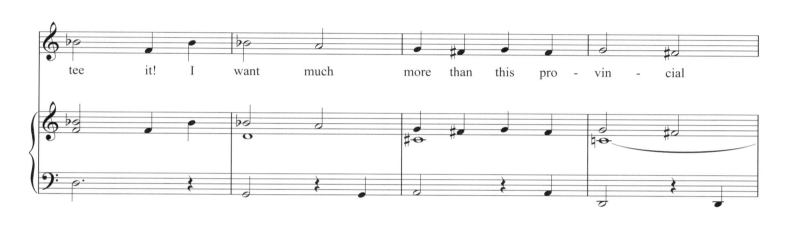

tee it! I want much more than this pro - vin - cial

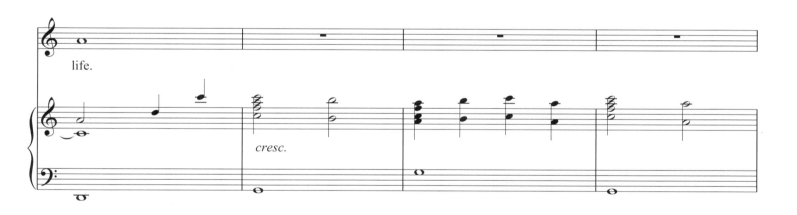

life.

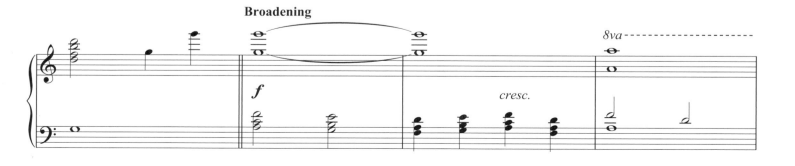

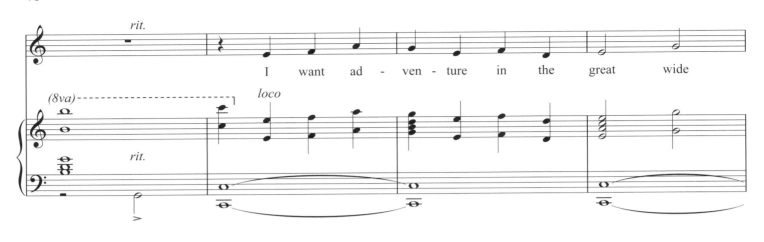

I want ad - ven - ture in the great wide

some - where! I want it more than I can tell!

And for once it might be grand to have some - one un - der -

stand. I want so much more than they've got planned.

A CHANGE IN ME

from Walt Disney's *Beauty and the Beast: The Broadway Musical*

Words by Tim Rice
Music by Alan Menken

22

HOME
from Walt Disney's *Beauty and the Beast: The Broadway Musical*

Music by Alan Menken
Lyrics by Tim Rice

INTO THE OPEN AIR

from the Walt Disney/Pixar film *Brave*

Words and Music by
Alexander L. Mandel

Moderate Folk Waltz

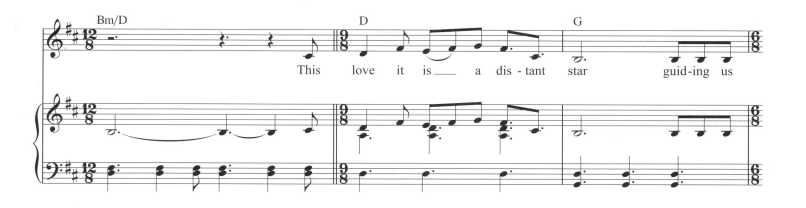

This love it is a dis-tant star guid-ing us

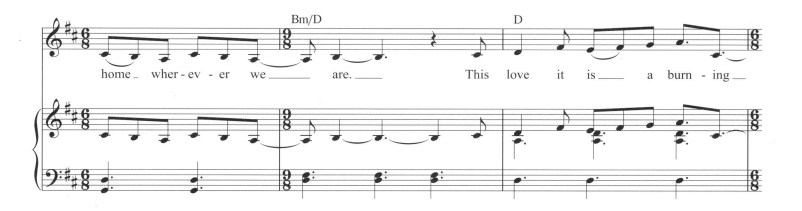

home wher-ev-er we are. This love it is a burn-ing

sun. Shine your light on the things that we've done. I

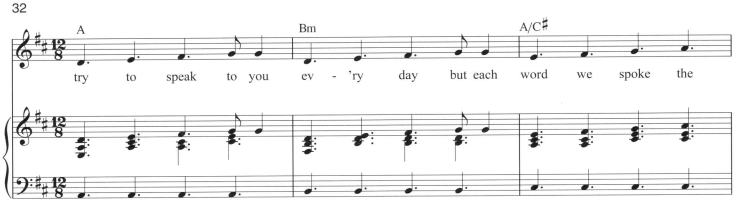

try to speak to you ev - 'ry day but each word we spoke the

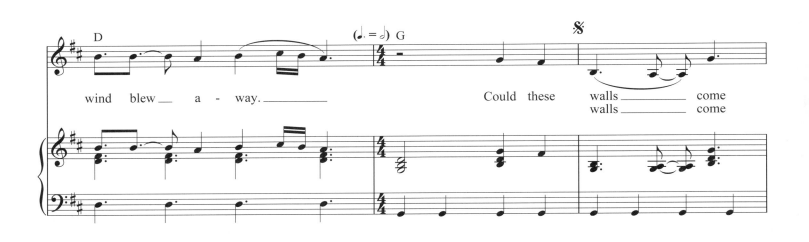

wind blew___ a - way.___ Could these walls_____ come
walls_____ come

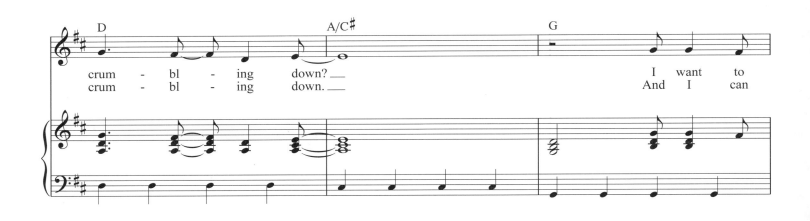

crum - bl - ing down?___ I want to
crum - bl - ing down.___ And I can

feel___ my feet___ on___ the ground_____
feel_____ my feet___ on___ the ground._____

and leave be - hind _____ this pris - on ___ we share. _
Can we car - ry ____ this love ___ that ___ we share ___

Step in - to the o - pen air. _

How did _____ we let ___ it come to this? _

TOUCH THE SKY
from the Walt Disney/Pixar film *Brave*

Music by Alexander L. Mandel
Lyrics by Alexander L. Mandel
and Mark Andrews

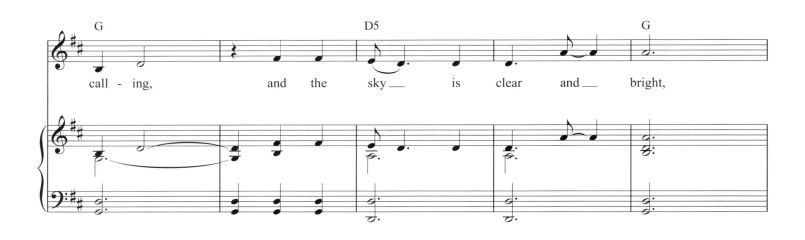

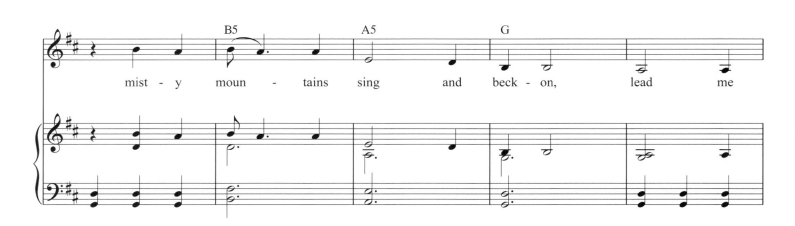

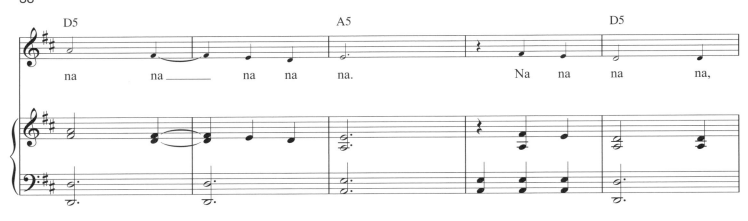

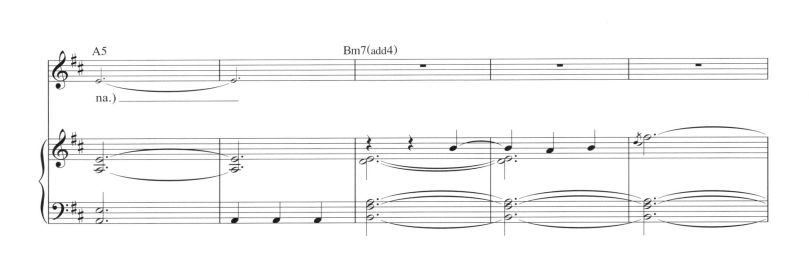

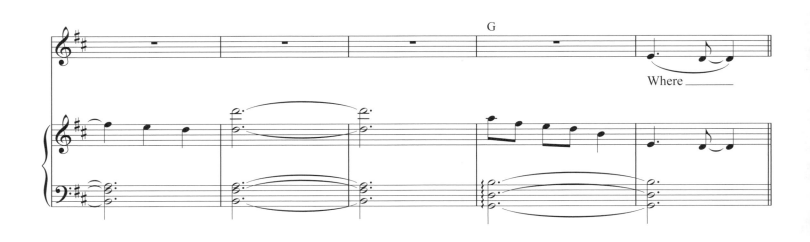

A DREAM IS A WISH YOUR HEART MAKES

from Walt Disney's *Cinderella*

Words and Music by Mack David,
Al Hoffman and Jerry Livingston

When I was a lit-tle girl, my fa-ther used to

say, if trou-ble ev-er trou-bles you, just dream your cares a-

way. A dream is a wish your heart makes ____

SO THIS IS LOVE
(The Cinderella Waltz)
from Walt Disney's *Cinderella*

Words and Music by Mack David,
Al Hoffman and Jerry Livingston

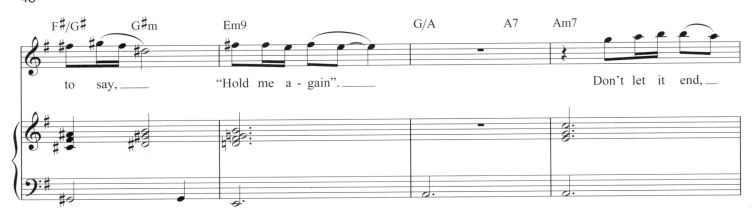

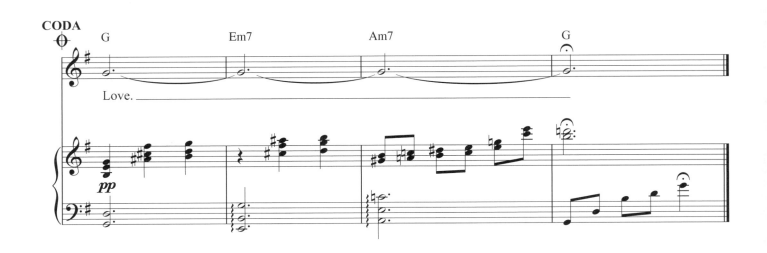

TRUE LOVE'S KISS
from Walt Disney Pictures' *Enchanted*

Music by Alan Menken
Lyrics by Stephen Schwartz

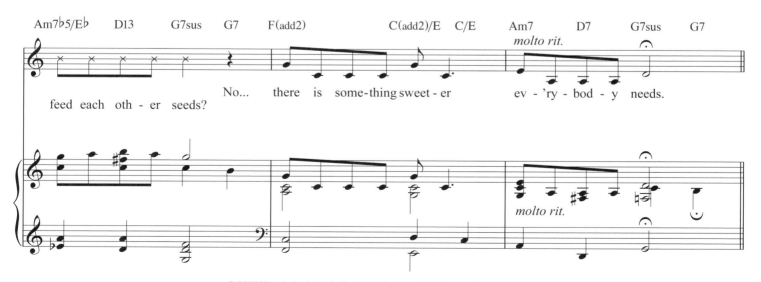

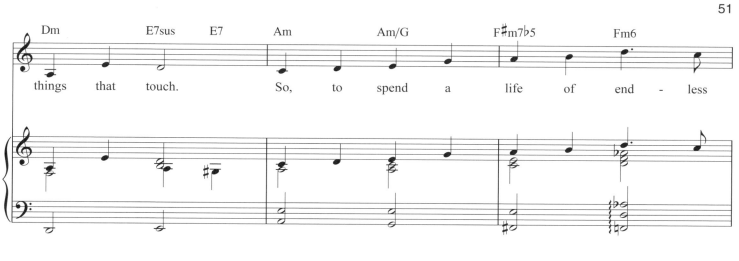

things that touch. So, to spend a life of end - less

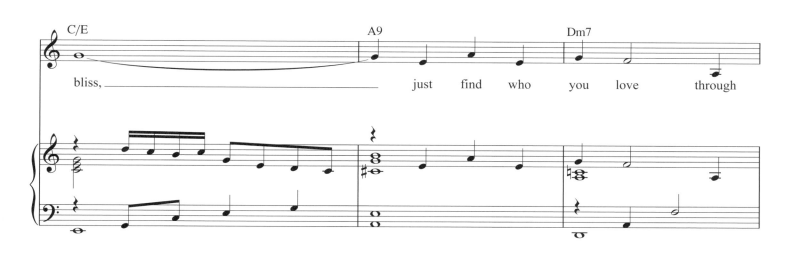

bliss, _____ just find who you love through

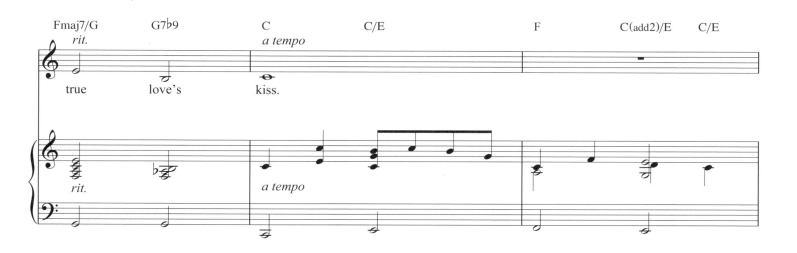

true love's kiss.

Light Waltz, in one

FOR THE FIRST TIME IN FOREVER

from Disney's Animated Feature *Frozen*

Music and Lyrics by Kristen Anderson-Lopez
and Robert Lopez

This song has been edited as a solo for this edition.

LET IT GO
from Disney's Animated Feature *Frozen*

Music and Lyrics by Kristen Anderson-Lopez
and Robert Lopez

Half-time feel, mysterious

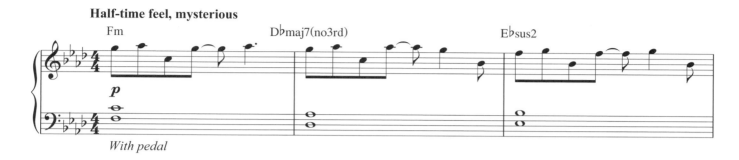

The snow glows white on the moun-tain to-night;__ not a

foot-print____ to be seen.__ A king-dom of i - so-la-

Gaining confidence

y - way.

It's fun - ny how some dis - tance makes ev - 'ry - thing__ seem small;__

__ and the fears that once__ con - trolled__ me can't

get to me__ at all.__ It's time__ to see__

what I __ can do, to test __ the lim - its and __ break through.

__ No right, __ no wrong, __ no rules __ for me, _____ I'm

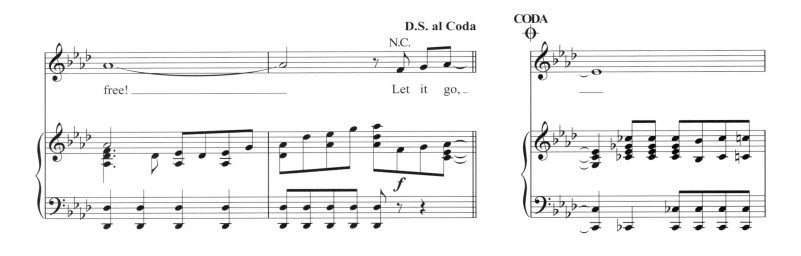

D.S. al Coda

CODA

free! _____ Let it go, _

I WON'T SAY
(I'm in Love)
from Walt Disney Pictures' *Hercules*

Music by Alan Menken
Lyrics by David Zippel

WHEN THERE WAS ME AND YOU
from the Disney Channel Original Movie *High School Musical*

Words and Music by
Jamie Houston

GOD HELP THE OUTCASTS

from Walt Disney's *The Hunchback of Notre Dame*

Music by Alan Menken
Lyrics by Stephen Schwartz

SOMEDAY
from Walt Disney's *The Hunchback of Notre Dame*

Music by Alan Menken
Lyrics by Stephen Schwartz

CAN YOU FEEL THE LOVE TONIGHT

from Disney Presents *The Lion King: The Broadway Musical*

Music by Elton John
Lyrics by Tim Rice

BEYOND MY WILDEST DREAMS

from Walt Disney's *The Little Mermaid - A Broadway Musical*

Music by Alan Menken
Lyrics by Glenn Slater

With excitement

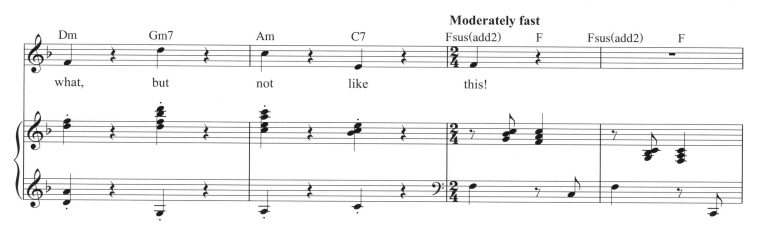

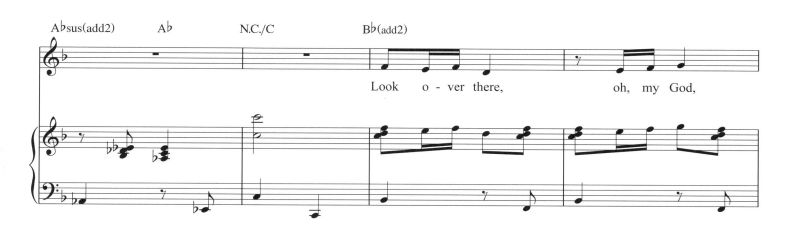

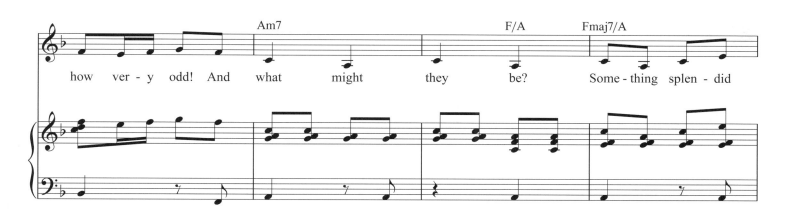

daz - zling, daz - ing, ut - ter - ly a - maz - ing!

Gaz - ing 'round, it's like to die! _____ Just

see - ing it feels so good, I'd scream, if I on - ly could! I'd

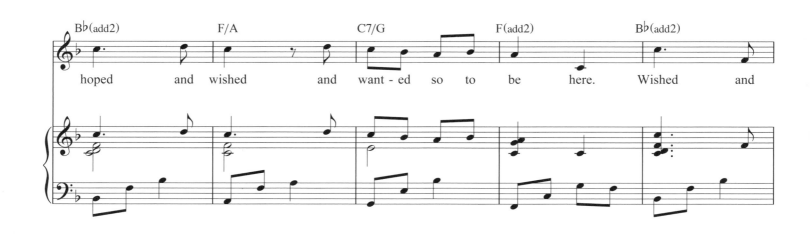

hoped and wished and want - ed so to be here. Wished and

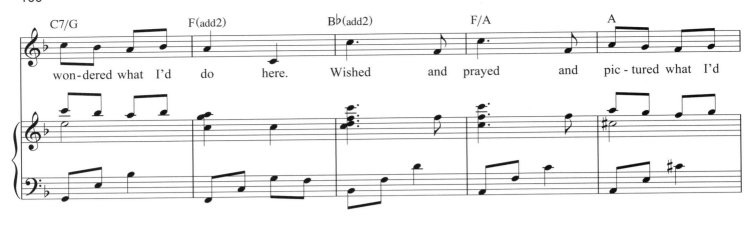

won-dered what I'd do here. Wished and prayed and pic-tured what I'd

see. Prayed, and wow! My pray'rs are com-ing true here.

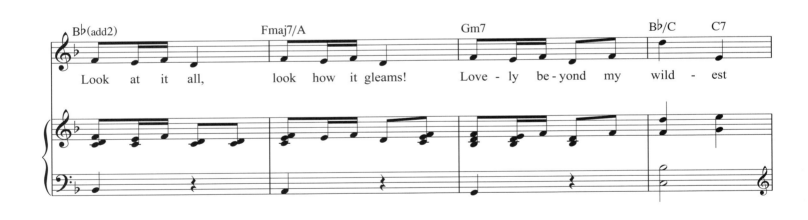

Look at it all, look how it gleams! Love-ly be-yond my wild-est

dreams.

PART OF YOUR WORLD

from Walt Disney's *The Little Mermaid - A Broadway Musical*

Music by Alan Menken
Lyrics by Howard Ashman

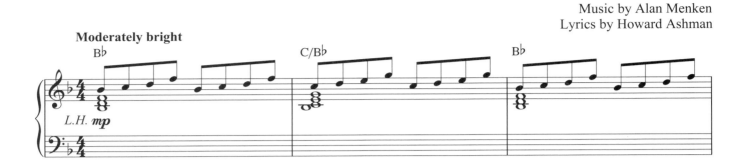

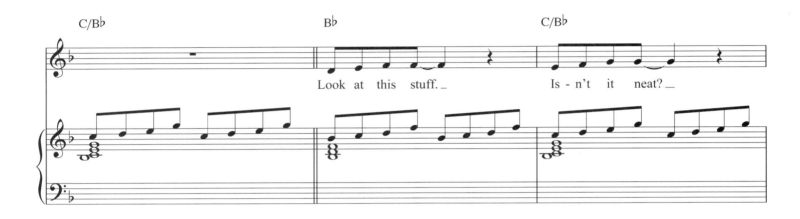

Look at this stuff. _ Is - n't it neat? _

Would-n't you think _ my col - lec-tion's com - plete? Would-n't you think _ I'm the girl, _

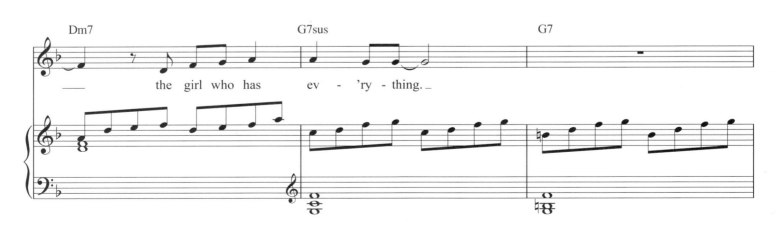

_ the girl who has ev - 'ry - thing.

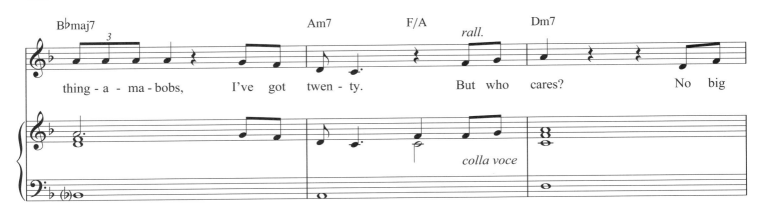

thing - a - ma - bobs, I've got twen - ty. But who cares? No big

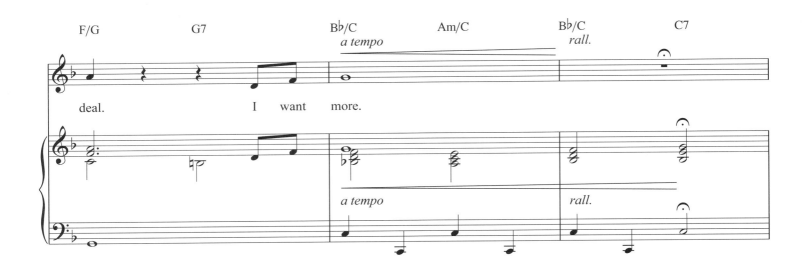

deal. I want more.

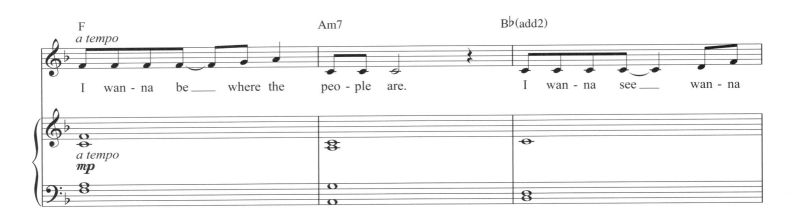

I wan - na be___ where the peo - ple are. I wan - na see___ wan - na

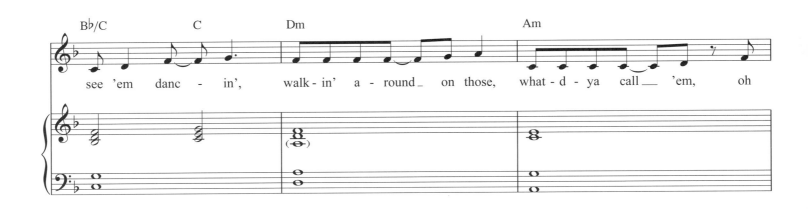

see 'em danc - in', walk - in' a - round___ on those, what - d - ya call ___ 'em, oh

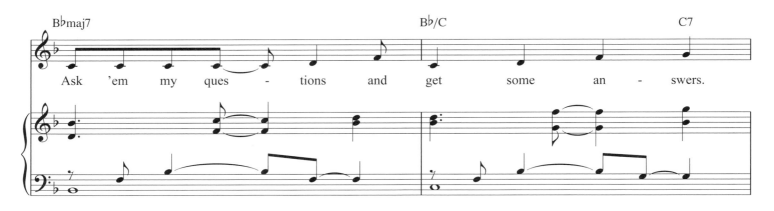

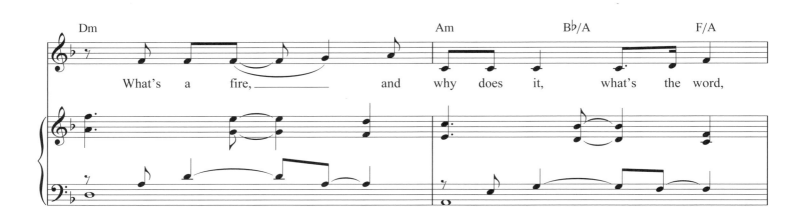

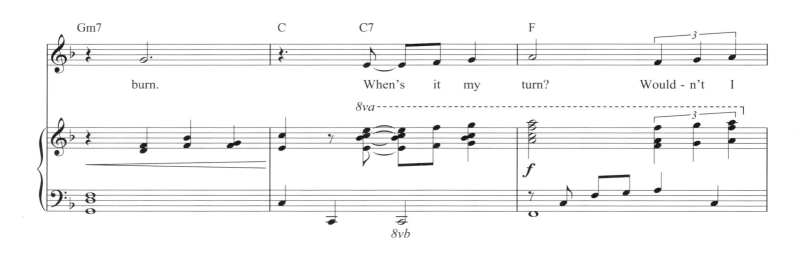

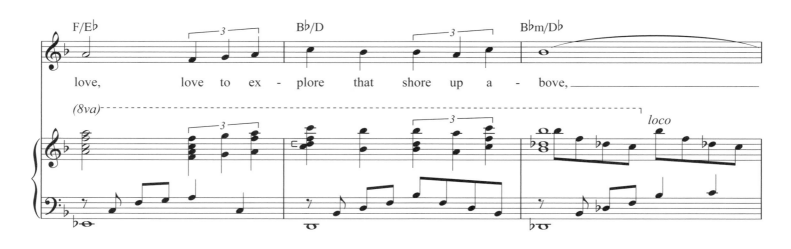

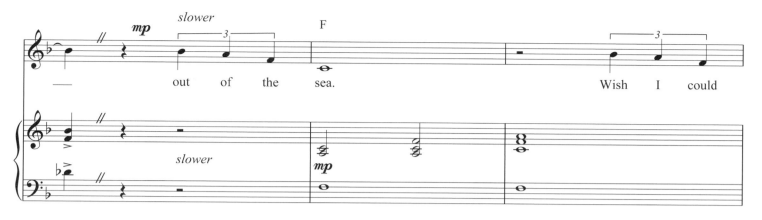

out of the sea.

Wish I could

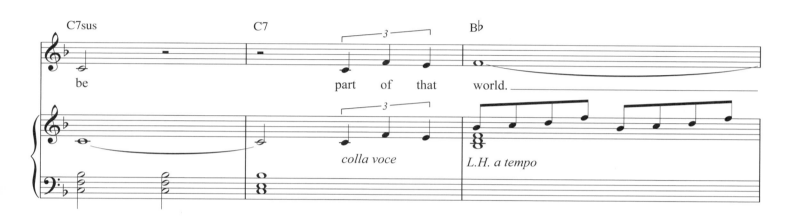

be

part of that world.

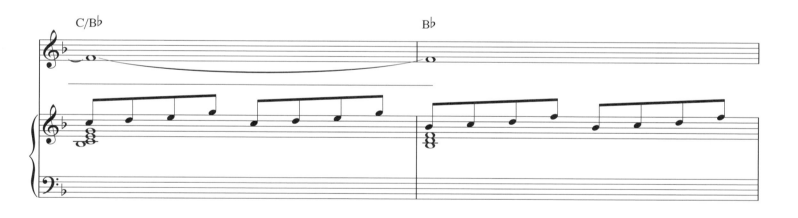

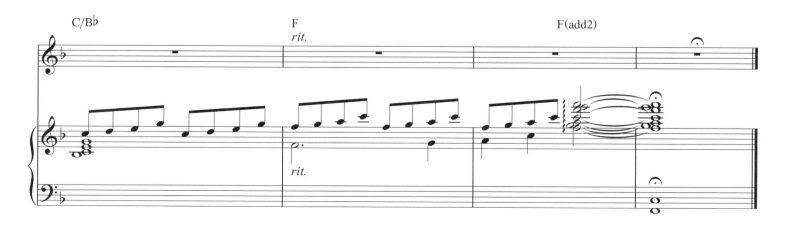

THE WORLD ABOVE

from Walt Disney's *The Little Mermaid - A Broadway Musical*

Music by Alan Menken
Lyrics by Glenn Slater

This is where I be-

long... be-neath the clear, wide blue here.

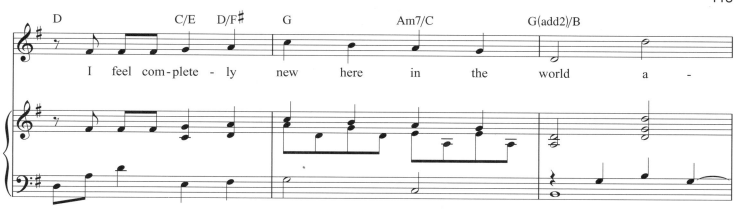

I feel com-plete-ly new here in the world a-

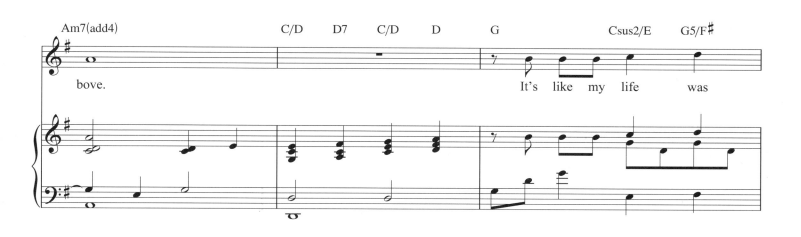

bove.   It's like my life was

wrong.   And some-how now at last I'm

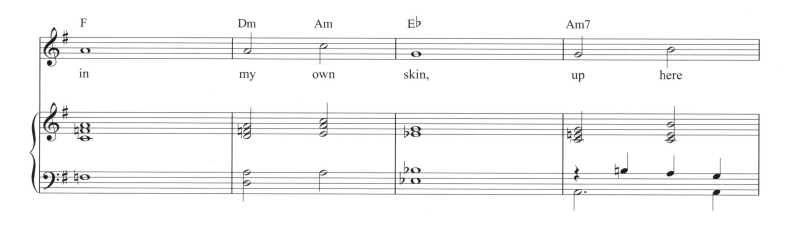

in   my   own   skin,   up   here

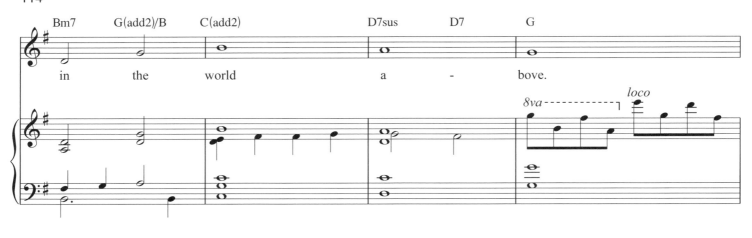

in the world a - bove.

There's so much light here,

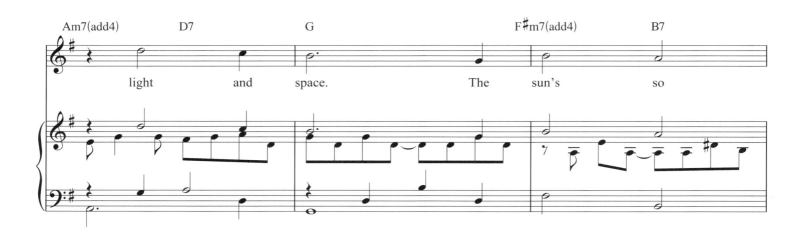

light and space. The sun's so

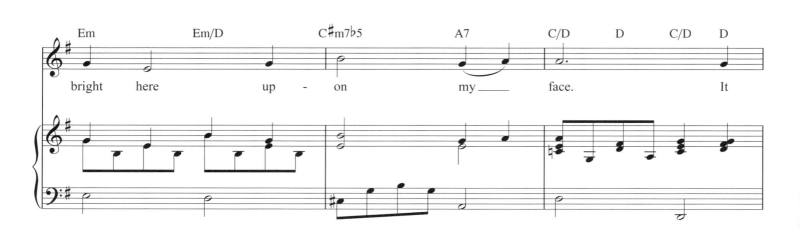

bright here up - on my ___ face. It

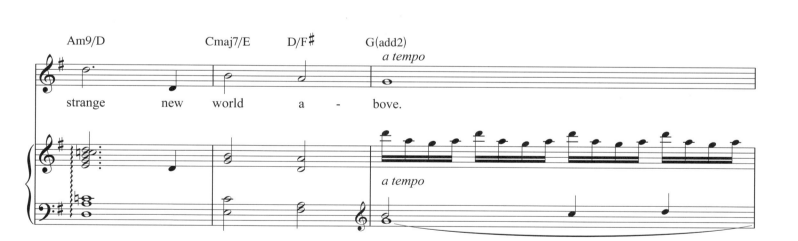

ANYTHING CAN HAPPEN

from *Mary Poppins*

Music by George Stiles
Lyrics by Anthony Drewe

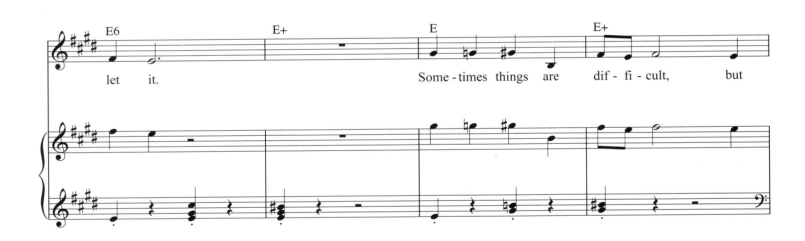

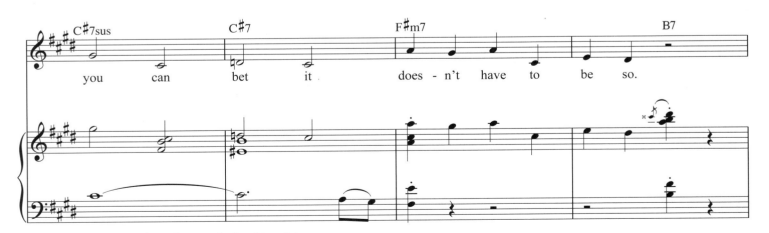

This song has been adapted as a solo for this edition.

yond fan - tas - tic. Dreams are made of

strong e - las - tic. Take some sound ad - vice and don't for -

get it. An - y - thing can hap - pen if you

let it.

FEED THE BIRDS
from Walt Disney's *Mary Poppins*

Words and Music by Richard M. Sherman
and Robert B. Sherman

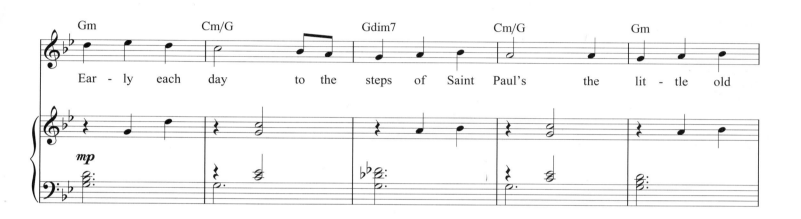

Ear - ly each day to the steps of Saint Paul's the lit - tle old

bird wom - an comes. _____ In her own spe - cial

way to the peo - ple she calls, "Come, buy my

PRACTICALLY PERFECT

from *Mary Poppins*

Music by George Stiles
Lyrics by Anthony Drewe

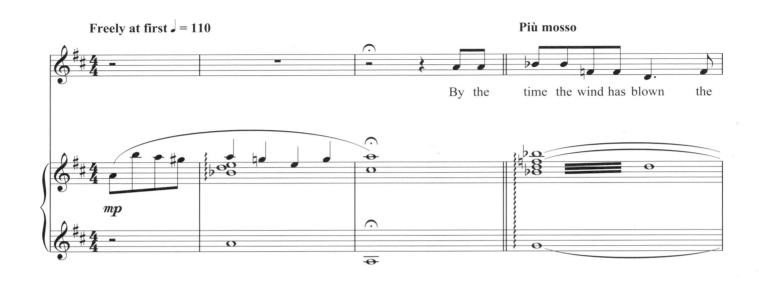

By the time the wind has blown the

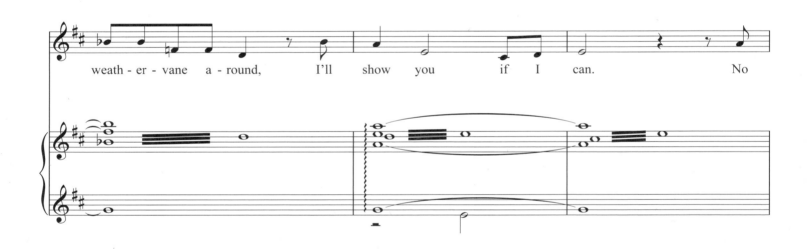

weath-er-vane a-round, I'll show you if I can. No

mat-ter what the cir-cum-stance, for one thing I'm re-nowned: my char-ac-ter is spit spot spick and

sound. I'm prac - ti-cal - ly per - fect _____ from head to

toe. If I had a fault, it would nev - er dare to

show. I'm so prac - ti - cal - ly per - fect in

Poco più mosso

ev - er - y way. _____

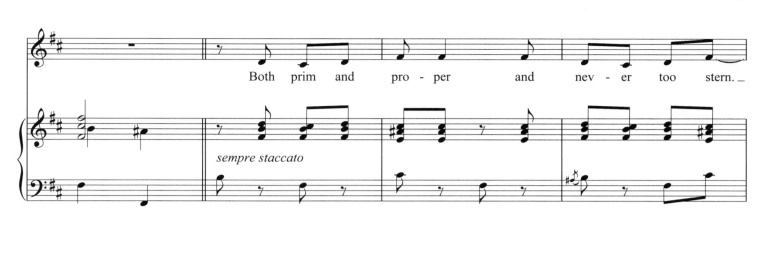

Both prim and pro - per and nev - er too stern.

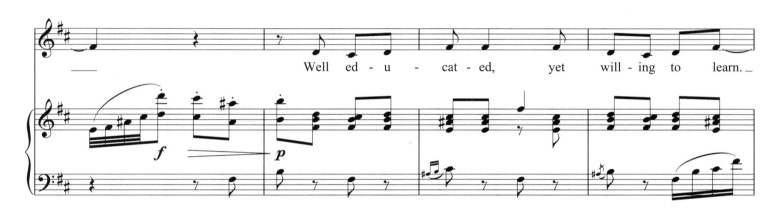

Well ed - u - cat - ed, yet will - ing to learn.

I'm clean and hon - est, my man - ner re - fined,

and I wear shoes of the sen - si - ble kind.

prac - ti - cal - ly per - fect, prac - ti -

cal - ly per - fect. You will be prac - ti - cal - ly

per - fect in ev - 'ry way.

A SPOONFUL OF SUGAR

from Walt Disney's *Mary Poppins*

Words and Music by Richard M. Sherman
and Robert B. Sherman

REFLECTION
from Walt Disney Pictures' *Mulan*

Music by Matthew Wilder
Lyrics by David Zippel

WATCH WHAT HAPPENS
from Walt Disney's *Newsies the Musical*

Music by Alan Menken
Lyrics by Jack Feldman

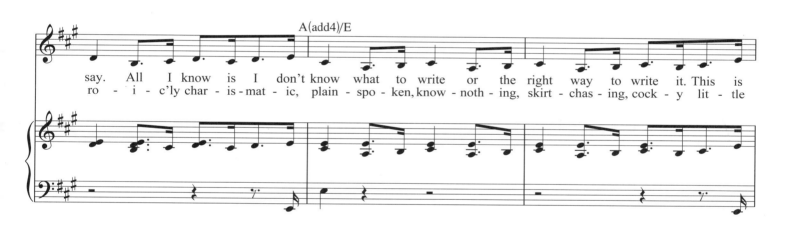

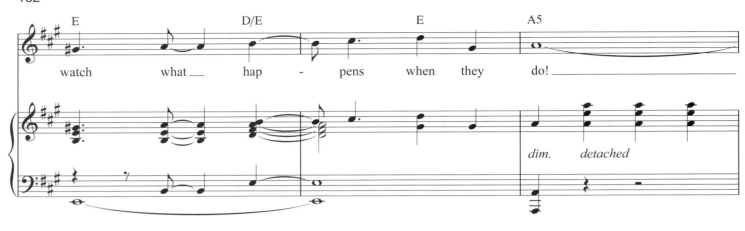

watch what __ hap - pens when they do! _____

D.S. al Coda

CODA

just give __ in. _____ It can't be __ an -

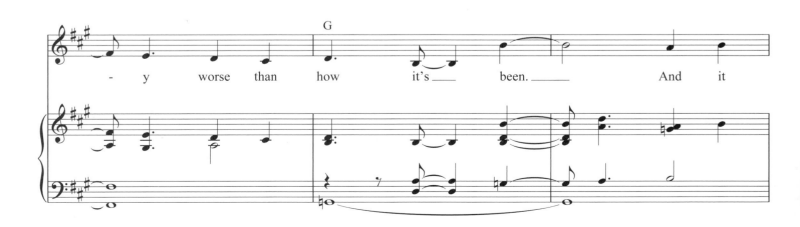

- y worse than how it's __ been. _____ And it

CANDLE ON THE WATER

from Walt Disney's *Pete's Dragon*

Words and Music by Al Kasha
and Joel Hirschhorn

I'll be your can-dle on the wa-ter,
I'll be your can-dle on the wa-ter

my love for you will al-ways
'til ev-'ry wave is warm and

burn.   I know you're lost   and drift-ing,   but the clouds are lift-ing.
bright.   My soul is there   be-side you,   let this can-dle guide you;

Don't give up; you have some-where to   turn.
soon you'll see a gold-en stream of   light.

THE SECOND STAR TO THE RIGHT

from Walt Disney's *Peter Pan*

Words by Sammy Cahn
Music by Sammy Fain

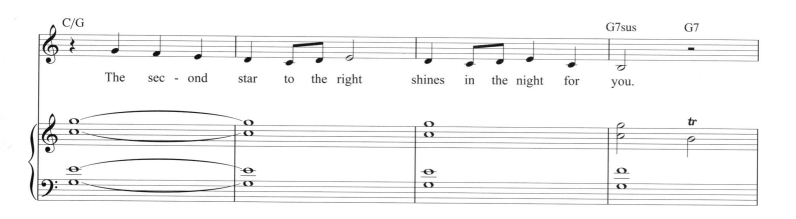

The sec - ond star to the right shines in the night for you.

to tell you that the dreams you plan real - ly can come true.

The sec - ond star to the right shines with a light that's

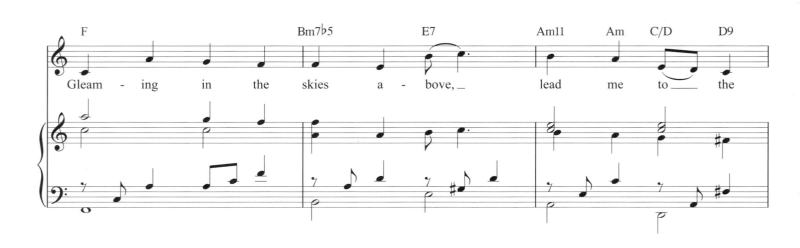

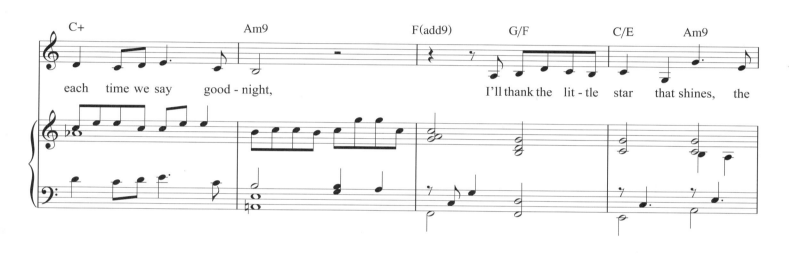

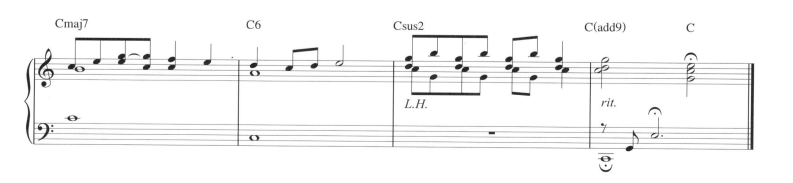

WHEN YOU WISH UPON A STAR

from Walt Disney's *Pinocchio*

Words by Ned Washington
Music by Leigh Harline

COLORS OF THE WIND

from Walt Disney's *Pocahontas*

Music by Alan Menken
Lyrics by Stephen Schwartz

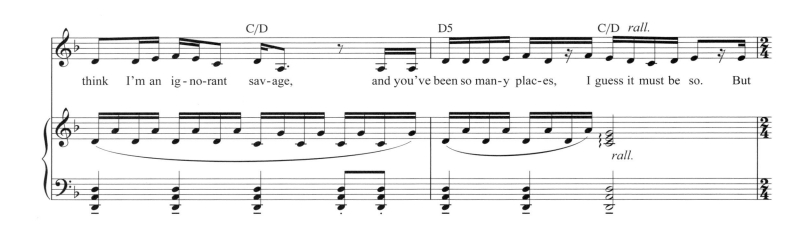

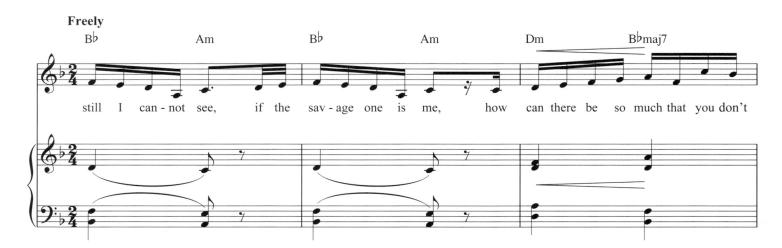

for - est, come taste the sun sweet ber - ries of the earth; come

roll in all the rich - es all a - round you, and for once nev - er won - der what they're

worth. The rain - storm and the riv - er are my broth - ers; the

her - on and the ot - ter are my friends; and we are all con - nect - ed to each

LE FESTIN
from Walt Disney Pictures' *Ratatouille* - A Pixar Film

Words and Music by Michael Giacchino
French Translation by Boualem Lamhene

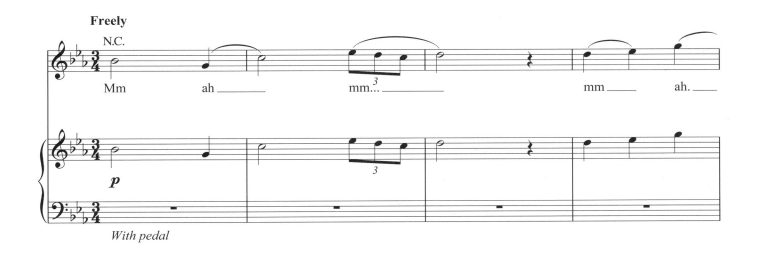

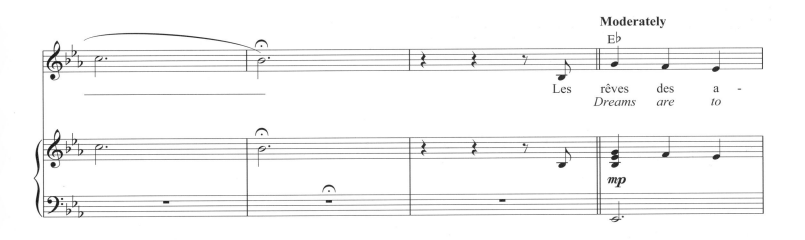

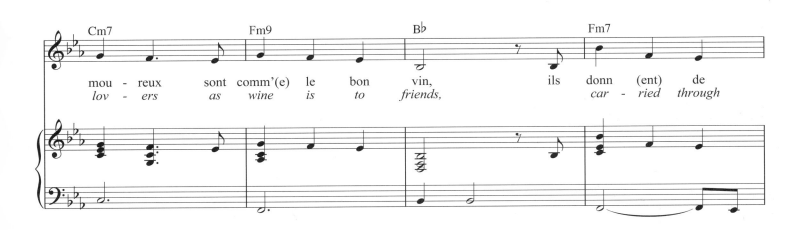

ONCE UPON A DREAM
from Walt Disney's *Sleeping Beauty*

Words and Music by Sammy Fain
and Jack Lawrence
Adapted from a Theme by Tchaikovsky

WITH A SMILE AND A SONG

from Walt Disney's *Snow White and the Seven Dwarfs*

Words by Larry Morey
Music by Frank Churchill

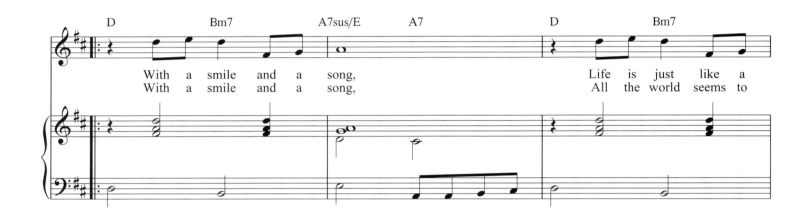

With a smile and a song,
With a smile and a song,

Life is just like a
All the world seems to

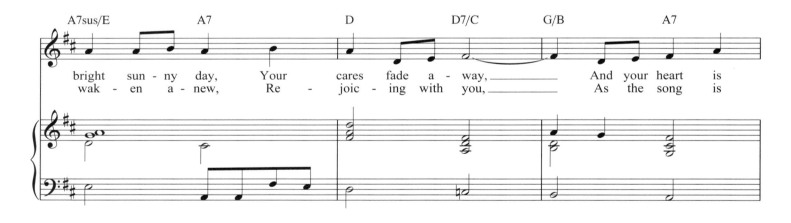

bright sun - ny day,   Your   cares fade a - way,_____   And your heart   is
wak - en a - new,   Re -   joic - ing with you,_____   As the song   is

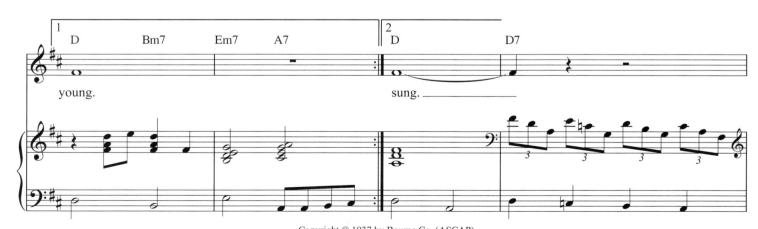

young.
sung._____

D.S. al Coda

I SEE THE LIGHT
from Walt Disney Pictures' *Tangled*

Music by Alan Menken
Lyrics by Glenn Slater

All those days, watch-ing from the win-dows.
Now I'm here, blink-ing in the star-light.

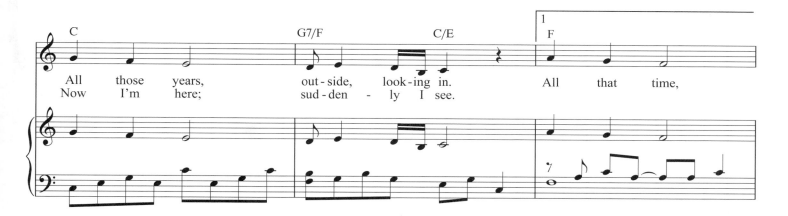

All those years, out-side, look-ing in.
Now I'm here; sud-den-ly I see.

All that time,

nev-er e-ven know-ing just how blind I've been.

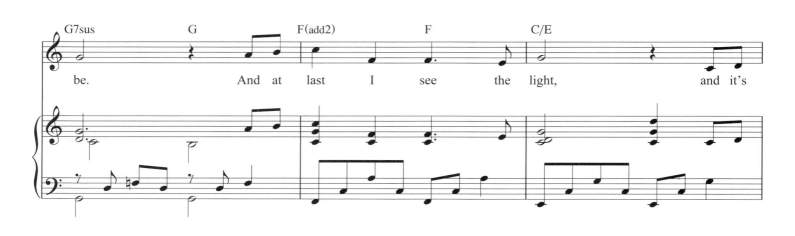

WHEN WILL MY LIFE BEGIN?

from Walt Disney Pictures' *Tangled*

Music by Alan Menken
Lyrics by Glenn Slater

Moderately fast Rock

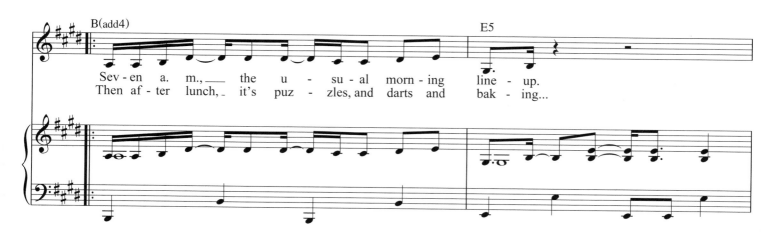

Sev - en a. m.,__ the u - su - al morn - ing line - up.
Then af - ter lunch,__ it's puz - zles, and darts and bak - ing...